The Temple Apprentice
From Tragedy to Triumph

Kay Stevick

TEACH Services, Inc.
PUBLISHING
www.TEACHServices.com • (800) 367-1844

World rights reserved. This book or any portion thereof may not be copied or reproduced in any form or manner whatever, except as provided by law, without the written permission of the publisher, except by a reviewer who may quote brief passages in a review.

The author assumes full responsibility for the accuracy of all facts and quotations as cited in this book. The opinions expressed in this book are the author's personal views and interpretations, and do not necessarily reflect those of the publisher.

This book is provided with the understanding that the publisher is not engaged in giving spiritual, legal, medical, or other professional advice. If authoritative advice is needed, the reader should seek the counsel of a competent professional.

Copyright © 2017 Kay Stevick

Copyright © 2017 TEACH Services, Inc.

ISBN-13: 978-1-4796-0799-0 (Paperback)

ISBN-13: 978-1-4796-0800-3 (Epub)

ISBN-13: 978-1-4796-0801-0 (Mobi)

Library of Congress Control Number: 2017914693

Scripture taken from the NEW AMERICAN STANDARD BIBLE®, Copyright © 1960, 1962, 1963, 1968, 1971, 1972, 1973, 1975, 1977, 1995 by The Lockman Foundation. Used by permission.

Scripture quotations marked KJV are taken from the King James Bible.

Scripture quotations taken from the 21st Century King James Version®, copyright © 1994. Used by permission of Deuel Enterprises, Inc., Gary, SD 57237. All rights reserved.

THE HOLY BIBLE, NEW INTERNATIONAL VERSION®, NIV® Copyright © 1973, 1978, 1984, 2011 by Biblica, Inc.® Used by permission. All rights reserved worldwide.

Scripture taken from the New King James Version®. Copyright © 1982 by Thomas Nelson. Used by permission. All rights reserved.

The ESV® Bible (The Holy Bible, English Standard Version®). ESV® Permanent Text Edition® (2016). Copyright © 2001 by Crossway, a publishing ministry of Good News Publishers. The ESV® text has been reproduced in cooperation with and by permission of Good News Publishers. Unauthorized reproduction of this publication is prohibited. All rights reserved.

The Holy Bible, English Standard Version (ESV) is adapted from the Revised Standard Version of the Bible, copyright Division of Christian Education of the National Council of the Churches of Christ in the U.S.A. All rights reserved.

Scripture marked RSV taken from the Revised Standard Version of the Bible, copyright © 1946, 1952, and 1971 the Division of Christian Education of the National Council of the Churches of Christ in the United States of America. Used by permission. All rights reserved.

The website references in this book have been shortened using a URL shortener and redirect service called 1ref.us, which TEACH Services manages. If you find that a reference no longer works, please contact us and let us know which one is not working so that we can correct it. TEACH Services is not responsible for the accuracy or permanency of any links.

Published by

TEACH Services, Inc.
P U B L I S H I N G
www.TEACHServices.com • (800) 367-1844

Table of Contents

Introduction. v

Chapter 1   Born of the Spirit 10

Chapter 2   A Time to Heal 16

Chapter 3   The Way to Live 34

Chapter 4   In His Image 42

Chapter 5   The Father's Will 47

Chapter 6   The Heart Made Flesh 52

Chapter 7   Walk With the Spirit. 55

Conclusion 57

Bibliography. 61

Introduction

An apprentice is defined as "a person who is learning a trade from a skilled employer, having agreed to work for a fixed period at low wages."[1] The disciples of the first century were in effect apprentices. They gave up their jobs to be healed and learn how to live. They had studied the Scriptures and had a deep need for deliverance from sin. When they saw Jesus, they recognized His service to them as something that could only be from God. Jesus's acknowledgement of their wounds and application of love, joy, peace, longsuffering, gentleness, goodness, faith, meekness, and temperance gave them an experience of blessing that they had only dared to hope for.

I've written this book to provide an experience that may be shared with others as a seven-part search of God's plan to give us a makeover. This plan to restore us includes everything that makes us human: the breath, the thoughts and emotions, and the will. Our brokenness may encounter the perfection of our Creator. This bonding with the Almighty picks up the pieces so we may live to heal and gather to God instead of clamoring and battering to defend ourselves, which separates us from God.

Jesus is our rescuer. The way out of this crushing world is the same as it was 2,000 years ago: to turn from the darkness to the light. This is the light of peace, peace that has the power to melt

---

[1] *Oxford Living Dictionaries*, s.v. "apprentice," http://1ref.us/kf (accessed August 3, 2017).

the hardest sinner, the peace of the cross. There is only one man who knows the way. Let us follow Him.

This book was written to help us to have an up close and personal experience with the Almighty. However, when you seek the truth about God, be prepared for it to be a chiseling process. This is what I experienced writing this book. It was my own experience of healing that helped me understand who God is and made it easy for me to speak of Him with others.

My mother used to say we should do our part to bring heaven to Earth as it says in the prayer the Savior gave us: "Thy will be done in earth, as it is in heaven" (Matt. 6:10, KJV). I believed this was important with all my heart. As a little child, I frequently experienced the pain and loneliness of being ill. I also experienced the peace and victory of being prayed for, the love and attention of my mother, the fortitude and faithfulness of my father.

We went to church regularly. I remember thinking I was experiencing heaven in the company and worship of those around me. Yet the conflict about what to believe raged in and around me and I continued to experience setbacks, in spite of the love that I knew was God.

Then the time came when influences near and far sent me reeling into the unknown: searching for more pieces of the fragmented truth that I loved. As my search has become increasingly unrelenting, I have come to realize that humans were made to be spiritual beings that demonstrate spiritual laws. Being made in the image of God means we were made for relationships—to portray the goodness of His judgment. Let us open this subject and dig as deep and long as it takes to find the treasure that Abba Yahweh has for us.

Apart from God, we are not spiritual. We are filled with life. Yet we become decayed, obsessed with ourselves and the people around us to the exclusion of God. We think we have faith as we fleetingly acknowledge God, but it is really unbelief. We need to examine ourselves so we may experience the fullness of belief separate from the fruits of brokenness—fear, shame, and bitterness.

When they are introduced to the Bible, people often shy away because it is known as a book of judgment. But we need truth, because we can't solve problems without judgment based on truth. Otherwise, we fall prey to wrong beliefs. The choice is between these beliefs and a different Holy God. Believing lies prevails in religious circles, whether worshipers believe lies about the Bible or other people. This is why people are wounded instead of healed at church. This book is written to show that the Bible is really a book about true love that heals—the Bible from God's perspective. It is a book with a plan. What gives God pleasure is our hoping that He will help us. Let us make a choice that this is the God we want to serve.

God's plan is revealed in the design and subjects of the temple of God: first in the tabernacle in the desert, then in the grand temple for God built by Solomon, and later the restored temple of Jesus's day. Jesus was the temple made flesh and as children of God, we also are temples made of flesh and blood.

Yes, the Bible is a holy Book. It is a book written to set us apart from the familiar that we may become better acquainted with God. The whole book is a revelation—a revelation for the apprentice, to show us that He truly is our Friend.

Gradually, I have learned to look at the Bible not by what I believe but what it says. One day, I was meditating on the sanctuary—the temples of the Bible, the tent in the desert, the building in Jerusalem, Jesus (the ultimate sanctuary), and the heavenly sanctuary. I was asking God, *What do you want to say here that is shrouded in confusion, yet is so powerfully, painfully plain that You went to all this painstaking detail and beauty to portray?* It is the image of God, the roles of the Father, Son, and Holy Spirit, to be reflected in the breath, the heart, and the will of every believer. This is the "plan of salvation," the blueprint of the temple.

The temple in its splendor is a display for true healthy living. We see the temple first in material form and then we admire the splendor of the temple in the flesh: Yahshua Jesus. God is so considerate. He explained to us ahead of time what was going to happen: Jesus was coming in the flesh with a pure heart to do the will of the Father with the wisdom of the Holy Spirit. The sanctuary was the ultimate prophecy. It spoke of the intimate encounter that Yahweh was preparing us for: the indwelling of His Spirit in us. This would occur not by power or might but by us willingly receiving His authority to work through our lives from the example of Jesus. The world conquers. Yahweh draws us with His yearning for us, the authority of His on-time, committed love.

> *Gradually, I have learned to look at the Bible not by what I believe but what it says.*

The earthly sanctuary was a herald of what God was going to do for us. This prepared us to understand that His plan was to not merely cover sin but to remove it by Yahshua's sacrifice. This is an internal cleansing of a symbolic blood transfusion and not only the external symbolic cleansing of water.

The first part of the Bible (or Old Testament) lays the foundation for the second part of the Bible (or New Testament). It prepares us to receive and appreciate the value of the sacrifice to be made. The Old Testament is not a mystery lost in the oblivion of religious exactions. The books of the Old Testament prepare us to be in awe, to begin to comprehend the character and works of the Son of God.

In this book, we will see that our being is meant to be the temple of the living God. The human body contains the breath, the heart, and the will. The material of the sanctuary always consisted of the best materials, such as gold, silver, jewels, and linen. This reflects the call to do the same for our bodies as the temples of the living God. Although this is vital to our condition, this book is focused on the breath, the heart, and the will. The breath, the heart, and the will make up the glory or character of each temple. We will see how the nature or image of God is reflected in the tabernacle that was first displayed in the wilderness, patterned after the heavenly sanctuary. It consists of the outer court, the Holy Place, and the Most Holy Place.

God's plan begins with the sacrifice that initiates our acceptance of God: the experience of being born of the Spirit. We will first take a close look at the "born again" experience provided by our Substitute. This will enable us to more fully value Him. We may then also be in a better position to spread the news of the gospel. For this we will need to understand the blood, the fire, and the water of the outer court.

Then we will consider the exchange that cures our hearts. Thus, we may love Him with our whole hearts and surrender our wills to Him. It is this, doing the will of the Father, that is the ultimate separation from the machinery of sin, as we walk in the fruit of the Spirit, bought and cleansed by the blood of the Lamb. At each phase of our walk with God, all three are available to mold and shape us into Their image.

Chapter 1
Born of the Spirit

"I will give you the keys of the kingdom of heaven."
Matthew 16:19 NASB

In this last generation, there has been a wealth of information about healing. Emotional healing is now widely accepted to be a critical part of optimal health. Even now there is a growing understanding of the importance of emotions in our wellness. Yet, this idea is not new. Several thousand years ago, God unfolded a health plan for the bewildered, embittered refugees from slavery, His people. It was called the sanctuary. This was a place of safety and true peace. The plan was to provide and demonstrate what was involved in healing and recovery. It addressed three keys to unlocking the mysteries of wellness—the breath, the heart, and the will. These are the guiding components of the being, the living body that makes us human. The sanctuary gives us a complete picture of the resources we need from God and what we can expect to find in the witnesses working for the Great Physician.

Every day we are jostled by the bustling schedule of our lives. Yet sometimes, we get a glimpse of another way to walk through life. Curious, thirsty, and fainting, we go to the nearest place of worship—only to be wounded and reeling, almost without hope. But our faith tells us, "Don't give up, there is more." For every murky representation of the truth, there is a robust, satisfying experience awaiting us.

The word *Bible* means different things to different people. The literal translation from the Greek word *biblia* means *books*.[2] The Bible is a library of the stories God wants us to understand and the very words of God Himself. Sometimes it is referred to as the Holy Book. *Holy* means *set apart* in Hebrew.[3] So, the Bible is a book about how to be set apart from the flood of chaos around us. Yes, this means you. This requires a plan—a covenant with God.

---

[2]Merriam-Webster's Student Dictionary, "Bible," http://1ref.us/kb (accessed August 3, 2017).
[3]Christian Crier, "What Does the Word Holy Mean?" http://1ref.us/kc (accessed August 3, 2017).

This covenant by blood is displayed in the sanctuary of the Bible. The covenant is also truly our protection.

We begin in the outer court of the sanctuary. What is in the outer court of the temple of God that makes it special? What is it that provides us with and teaches us about wellness? It is our acceptance by God. We see that God is concerned about us and He wants to relate to us. Here we learn of the three ways the Almighty uses to draw us to Himself: blood, fire, and water.

When we go into the outer court, on the altar we see the physical blood representing that of the Son of man and God. This is necessary to crack the complacent darkness of daily living that engulfs almost every thought, word, and deed. We ask God to forgive us and we acknowledge the need for the Sacrifice in our lives. The fire of the Spirit consumes the death in our lives. Then we are free to desire to do the will of the Father and to cleanse our lives at the basin of water. The outer court is a representation of the born-again experience. This is the first part of the plan of salvation. Thus, we are prepared to learn the ways to feed the spirit and starve the flesh.

In the outer court, we are introduced to the concerned God. Yahshua's blood takes away our sin. We meet the Holy Spirit in the form of fire. The very fiery breath of life consumes the sin offering, that we may approach the Holy Places—the Holy Place and the Most Holy Place. The cleansing will of the Father is represented by the water. Here, for the first time, we experience God with us.

This is where we may lead someone to the born-again experience. Describe the components. Show that being born of the Spirit is a covenant-contract with God. He supplies everything. We just need to do the small but critical part of giving Him our willingness, opening the door. This is the beginning of a health exchange where the Doctor gives you His health.

God made Adam and Eve with the fruit of the Spirit. But when they sinned they no longer had direct access to this fruit. By faith in the works of Jesus, we again have access to the tree of life. We may share in God's goodness and eternal life by partaking of the fruit of the Spirit. We still need to heed the admonition to not eat of the tree of good mixed with evil. Even as Christians who believe in the promises of God, are we still trembling at the thought of not having our fruit from the tree of good and evil?

God reinstated His covenant made in Eden with the offering of sacrifice. Jesus was willing to live everyday life. He was also willing to meet the cross where He sacrificed Himself and became part human forever. May we be willing to make sacrifices to remain true to our personal convictions and leave the consequences to the Father. Jesus came to the Father on His own merit. We come to the Father not on our own works but on Jesus's works. His works did earn salvation because they were without sin and were always based on obeying the Father's will and trusting the consequences to the Father's care.

When we want to stress a person's worth, we often say that he or she is the salt of the earth. In the ancient world, salt was highly valued. The Christian's task is to be the salt of society: preserving, reconciling, adding taste, giving meaning where there is no meaning, giving hope where there is no hope. This is the salt of the earth, peace with the Father, the example of the Son and the fruit of the Spirit. It is with the blessings that come from having a covenant with God that we have hope for real, lasting bonds with each other.

Keep the covenant—don't lose it. Be willing to live the commandments, because this is how God guides your life. Hold on to the wealth of the covenant, the fruit of the Spirit. This takes away the pressure to make things happen. We just need to be willing to receive patience, love, goodness, and joy from God to share with others who are in the moment with us. As these qualities are sealed into our hearts, a solid foundation is formed on which we can continuously minister to the brokenhearted and the downtrodden to distribute the covenant wealth. Such is the life sustained by the covenant. The covenant plan is simply that God gives us His riches for our rags because of what Jesus did.

The sanctuary is a display of the covenant. As we look at the parts of it, we see that God is interested in all of us—the heart, the breath, and the will. He wants to deliver us from the effects of sin and He also wants to sustain us apart from sin, without spot or wrinkle.

> *The covenant plan is simply that God gives us His riches for our rags because of what Jesus did.*

If we will understand the grandeur and expansiveness of the principles of everlasting life, we will be prepared to accept them and be sealed into service for the heavenly kingdom. The covenant has resources that are based on the radical physical creation that we are placed in by God—a way that includes security, comfort, and beauty. Would you want it any other way? So, why don't we stop trying to tell God what to do and listen to what has been bothering Him and what He wants to do about it?

All of God is with us in each phase of our apprenticeship: the Father, the Son, and the Holy Spirit. So we need to begin to get to know the Almighty by identifying the components of the glory that is God. We are made in the image of this glory: the heart, the breath, and the will.

Yahweh not only heals our hearts and gives us purpose by sharing His will, He also gives us the Breath of Life to strengthen and encourage us. What a plan! In the Garden, when Adam and Eve sinned, they separated themselves from this precious Fire and this is what began the process of decay. But then there was the plan to make everything right again.

Understanding the sanctuary is one of the keys to having the privilege of one day going into the Garden of Eden. It is here that we discover what Yahshua Jesus did for us. The fire at the gate no longer keeps us out. In the outer court we see that the fire consumes the sacrifice of the Lamb of God instead of us. Thus, we may safely enter the Holy Place. Here, we have access to the example of the Son of God. He shows us the way back to everlasting life—to the Most Holy Place—back to company with the angels and the fiery presence of God. It is that simple! Is it only hell that is fire? No, no, no. Heaven is also fiery. The difference is those that burn up in the fires of hell don't want to relate to the Substitute. Let us receive the nature of God by the blood, the fire, and the water.

Chapter 2
A Time to Heal

"I will restore you to health and I will heal you of your wounds, declares the Lord."
Jeremiah 30:17 NASB

Leviticus is the book that gives us the sanctuary services. The Hebrew word for Leviticus means *and He called*.[4] We may ask, "Why is He calling?" God is in one place and we are in another place. The Father is calling us to grow in the plan of salvation: to come join Him so He can make even our homes a blessing.

God is calling us to be loved. The pagan religions of the past and present make sacrifices to get the gods to do something. Thus, manipulation by fear, anger, and guilt, to trust in something that is a curse, is the way of the world. This is the power of witchcraft. We know better. We read the words *pagan*, *heathen*, *gentiles*. They are designations for people in the world that live without the blessings of knowing the true God. Yes, the ways of the past are alive and well in the twenty-first century. The ancient traditions have drawn even Christians to their ceremonies. It is with an understanding of the sanctuary that we may begin to separate from the ties to warcraft that are just as alive and well today as any time in the past. Truly, we have a need to understand the way out that our God, Yahweh, has provided.

We learn more about the Creator's plan to restore our nature by moving into the Holy Place of the sanctuary. What is in the Holy Place that makes it special? What is it that provides for and teaches us about wellness?

First and foremost, the Holy Place is a private place. We go from the public outer court through the warm, rich draperies that enshroud the private beauty of the entrance to the presence of God. Inside, we see representations of the ministry Yahweh uses to heal our hearts. The table of bread symbolizes Jesus, who became the Bread of Life that gives us strength by dying for us. The bread of His presence on the table represents the oneness with God and

---

[4]"*Vayikra*, 'And He Called': How Can a Book Start with 'And'?" http://1ref.us/kg (accessed August 3, 2017).

the fellowship we may have with each other. The candlestick represents the Spirit, who sheds light in the darkness so that we can see. The altar of incense, before the Most Holy Place, represents Yahshua Jesus's prayers to the Father to do His will. These are the instruments that are used to heal our hearts that we may love the Lord our God with all our heart and strength.

First, we will look at what Jesus did and why we need His heart. The covenant exchange is our hearts for His. So, we will ask for the Holy Spirit to shed light into our hearts to examine our hearts so we may be willing to be healed. Next, we will see how the golden lamps represent the Spirit who sheds light. Prayer is the time when we relate to the Father.

The Bread

Sin allures, then opens a trapdoor or wraps us in chains. We end up looking for ways to quiet the conscience instead of how to maintain the great peace that comes from being impressed with God. The Bible raises a barrier between us and the world and its traps. The sanctuary calls us out of the trouble we are in. The greatest call comes from the life of Yahshua. Jesus's life revealed that He would rather have His will surrendered, His heart broken and body sacrificed, than to make a break from the Father, to live without the fruit of the Spirit. This same life is available to us today. As we look at Jesus's life, we recognize that the circumstances of our own lives were met with the rich blessings of the Bread of Life.

Yahshua Jesus

went to where we were
taught forgiveness
was content in the outdoor elements
used what was near at hand from the earth
showed us the way to be heavenly

His food was simple
He walked a lot
He worked His area of the world, planted seeds,
then would leave and come back
kept the disciples close and loved them, even when they erred
did not always volunteer the things of God
sometimes said as little as possible with tears in His voice
believed the "impossible"
valued our restoration
spoke to the Father on our behalf
touched people
ate with people
understood and recognized our hurts and weaknesses
opposed the false
Jesus shared the Father and the Holy Spirit

The only one who can satisfy our needs is the One who made us. It has been now close to seven thousand years and He is the only one to show us how to truly live! What Jesus gives us is the fruit of keeping the law. Jesus' gift is the only way we can obey and have love, joy, peace, longsuffering, gentleness, goodness, faith, meekness, and temperance, because it is impossible for us to keep the law.

The only one who can satisfy our needs is the One who made us.

The Golden Lamps

The Golden Lamps of the Holy Place represent the Holy Spirit giving us light on our Savior and the fruit of the Spirit. Next, we see that He used the love languages that produced the fruit of the Spirit. He truly is the Bread of Life. My prayer is that you may have a glimpse of the magnificence of what Jesus did for us. The main themes of the Bible are all tied together in our Savior, the Ten Commandments, our brokenness, and the will of the Father. The Son of God came in the flesh to die for our sins. Jesus also came as the Son of man so that the fruit of the Spirit could be wrought in human flesh by His addressing our brokenness.

How did Jesus respond to brokenness? How did He heal the hearts of His disciples? We will also examine the lives of the disciples and see how the Savior healed them by living by the laws of life. His use of the love languages produced the fruit of the Spirit. By experiencing the attributes or love languages of God, people were able to experience closeness to God and have their hope and faith revived. Jesus truly is the Bread of Life.

Depression

Philip told Nathanael to come and see the Lord. But Nathanael was not so sure. Nathanael approached the Savior with depression. He said to Philip, "Can any good thing come out of Nazareth?" (John 1:46, NASB). The Son of God responds with affirmation. Jesus saw Nathanael coming and said, "Behold, an Israelite indeed, in whom there is no deceit" (John 1:47, NASB). Jesus met Nathanael's depression by recognizing Nathanael's honesty. When Nathanael had this intimate response from Jesus, he answered with joy in his heart, "Rabbi, You are the Son of God; You are the King of Israel" (John 1:49, NASB).

The first commandment of God is this: "You shall have no other gods before Me" (Exod. 20:3, NASB). God was speaking to the Israelites in terms that they could understand. There is a universal law of life that God wanted to use to protect them. This is the law of beholding: We become like what we behold. Whatever we look at, with or without God, is binding in our lives. This law is also found in 2 Corinthians 3:18: "But we all, with unveiled face, beholding as in a mirror the glory of the Lord, are being transformed into the same image from glory to glory, just as from the Lord, the Spirit" (NASB). When we keep this commandment, we experience the fruit of the Spirit—joy.

Fear

The next story of brokenness—found in John 21—is about when Peter and some disciples were meeting together. Peter decided he should go fishing. His friends decided to go too. It turned out that they didn't catch any fish. But then as the light of day began to dawn, someone called from shore asking if they had any fish. They told him no. Next, the person on shore told them to put the net on the other side of the boat. Then the nets were full to breaking. John shouted, "It is the Lord" (John 21:7, NASB). Flabbergasted, Peter jumped into the sea. He wanted to hide from Jesus because he was afraid what Jesus would say to him. When Jesus was taken to be crucified, Peter cursed and denied his relationship with Jesus. Later, when Jesus said, "Bring some of the fish which you have now caught" (John 21:10, NASB), Peter emerged from the water to get back in the boat to obey the command. He had not raced ahead to get to Jesus (John 21:11, NIV).

After meeting his economic and physical needs, Yahshua addressed Peter's emotional need. At the heart of Peter's fear was his wanting Jesus to know that he loved Him. Jesus knew this and therefore asked, "Simon, son of Jonas, lovest thou me?" (John 21:15, KJV). Jesus then bestowed the gift of honor by asking Peter to tend His sheep (John 21:15). Peter understood that he had inherited the calling from Jesus. This gave him great peace as we see that when Jesus told him of the manner of his death, Peter did not respond rashly. He remained submissive and was content with the inheritance: "Feed my sheep" (John 21:16, KJV). Although Peter's fear led him to deny Jesus, Jesus said Peter would gain victory over fear to the point he would allow himself to die on a cross (John 21:18–19).

The second commandment says, "You shall not make for yourself an idol, or any likeness of what is in heaven above or on the earth beneath it or in the water under the earth. You shall not worship them or serve them; for I, the Lord your God, am a jealous God, visiting the iniquity of the fathers on the children, on the third and the fourth generations of those who hate Me, but showing lovingkindness to thousands, to those who love Me and keep My commandments" (Exod. 20:4–6, NASB). This is the law of inheritance: Blessings, as well as behavior patterns, curses, and strongholds, are passed down from generation to generation. We reap the good inheritance only because of what Christ sowed. This law is also found in Colossians 1:12–14: "Giving thanks to the Father, who has qualified us to share in the inheritance of the saints in Light. For He rescued us from the domain of darkness, and transferred us to the kingdom of His beloved Son, in whom we have redemption, the forgiveness of sins" (NASB). When we worship only God and eliminate service to false authorities, we have the fruit of the Spirit—peace.

Resentment

The definition of resentment is "a feeling of indignant displeasure or persistent ill will at something regarded as a wrong, insult, or injury."[5]

There is a story in the book of Mark about a man who ended up filled with unclean spirits. He lived in a graveyard and cut

---

[5] *Merriam-Webster Online*, s.v. "resentment," http://1ref.us/kd (accessed August 3, 2017).

himself with rocks. But when he saw Jesus, he ran toward Him and bowed at His feet.

But this man with unclean spirits spoke words of resentment. Jesus recognized this as fallen spirits and delivered the man from them. Then the saved man was faithful and witnessed to the power of God in his community, as Jesus asked him to do (Mark 5:1–20). We see that with every intervention of Yahshua Jesus there is a facet of the fruit of the Spirit that becomes present in the life of the healed.

The third commandment is this: "You shall not take the name of the Lord your God in vain" (Exod. 20:7, NASB). This is the law of witness: When we take the name of Christian, we bear either a true or a false witness to who He is.

Shame

In the book of Luke, Jesus tells a story about a young man who wasted the resources that his father gave him. When the wealth was all gone, he realized how misguided he was and decided to go back and ask his father for work.

The once reckless son returned to his father, filled with shame. It was because he knew his father was faithful to God and would accept him back that the son had the courage to return. The father responded to the shame in the son's heart by spending quality time with him by holding a feast. The shame was removed and the healing complete. The young man was no longer disobedient but able to be fully obedient to his father (Luke 15:11–32).

The fourth commandment is this: "Remember the Sabbath day, to keep it holy" (Exod. 20:8, NKJV). This is the law of faith: The Sabbath and its blessing is received by the obedience of faith. This is also found in Hebrews 4:4–11: "For He has said somewhere concerning the seventh day: 'And God rested on the seventh day from all His works' … So there remains a Sabbath rest for the people of God. For the one who has entered His rest has himself also rested from his works, as God did from His. Therefore let us be diligent to enter that rest, so that no one will fall, through following the same example of disobedience" (NASB). It is by the law of faith in God that we may have the fruit of obedience.

Desire for Control

One day, the disciples and Jesus were walking to Capernaum. Apparently, Jesus was left alone, even while walking with His disciples. Jesus asked them, "What were you discussing on the way?" (Mark 9:33). The disciples were quiet because they had discussed who would be the greatest in the kingdom of heaven. They knew it was wrong. Jesus said it was by acts of caring that they would reap the rewards of the law of sowing and reaping. Then He showed them that it was kindness, such as caring for the needs of a child, that had its highest reward (Mark 9:33–37).

The fifth commandment is this: "Honor your father and mother, that your days may be prolonged in the land which the Lord your God gives you" (Exod. 20:12, NASB). This is the law of sowing and reaping: Whether we think our parents deserve respect or not, this is a command from God. He is the one who promises to keep us, to make it work. This law is also found in Galatians 6:8: "For the one who sows to his own flesh will from the flesh reap corruption, but the one who sows to the Spirit will from the Spirit reap eternal life" (NASB). When we honor the law of sowing and reaping, we will live by the fruit of the Spirit—kindness.

Anger

After Jesus and His remaining eleven disciples finished the Last Supper, the Master took them to a quiet garden. It was there that Judas brought the group of agitated men who were ordered to bring Him to the high priest. Peter immediately assumed that the will of Jesus was for him to defend Him, by cutting off the high priest's servant's ear. No, Jesus did not want Peter to be critical of Malchus. So He put back Malchus's ear and told Peter to put his sword back. Jesus asked Peter, "Shall I not drink the cup which My Father has given Me?" (John 18:1–11, NKJV). It wasn't just a command with which Jesus responded to Peter, it was also with a question. When a person is being critical, pray for discernment for the right question to ask that will lead them to a quiet understanding, that they may be patient.

The sixth commandment says, "You shall not murder" (Exod. 20:13, NASB). This is the law of judging: Jesus said, "You have heard that the ancients were told, 'You shall not commit murder' and 'Whoever commits murder shall be liable to the court.' But I say to you that everyone who is angry with his brother shall be guilty before the court" (Matthew 5:21–22, NASB). If we are to keep this law, we must have the fruit of the Spirit—patience.

A Sense of Rejection

Jesus had been on the Mount of Olives in prayer to His Father. Then He went early in the morning to the temple, where the people would gather to hear Him. As the gentle rays of the morning sun warmed those in the court of the temple, angry men brought a trembling woman to Jesus.

Jesus used gentleness to address the angry men and merely wrote their sins in the sand. He stood between the woman and the men to protect the woman caught in adultery. Her accusers wanted Jesus to reject her too. But she was able to experience protection from the Savior (John 8:1–11). The seventh commandment says, "You shall not commit adultery" (Exod. 20:14, NASB). This is the law of loyalty: Our commitment is based on the other person's welfare, not on our own. Duty of loyalty is a term used "in corporation law to describe a fiduciary's 'conflicts of interest and requires fiduciaries to put the corporation's interests ahead of their own.'"[6] This law is also found in Matthew—Jesus said loyalty means 100 percent. His words were, "You have heard that it was said, 'You shall not commit adultery'; but I say to you that everyone who looks at a woman with lust for her has already committed adultery with her in his heart" (Matt. 5:27–28, NASB). To keep this commandment, we must have the fruit of the Spirit—gentleness.

Self-Reliance

In the book of Luke, we read about a tax collector named Zacchaeus. Apparently, he took advantage of his position of authority and asked more than was required from the citizens. Zacchaeus was depending on himself to meet his needs, but he was stealing from others. Jesus knew that what he needed was to get the focus off his personal needs and meet someone else's needs. So He told Zacchaeus that He must stay at his home. Touched by Jesus's transparency and shared need, Zacchaeus gave half of his possessions to the poor and returned four times what he had stolen (Luke 19:1–10).

The eighth commandment is this: "You shall not steal" (Exod. 20:15, NASB). This is the law of giving: We need to be sensitive to what we owe to others. This law is also found in Luke 6:38, which says, "Give, and it will be given to you" (NASB). As you give, so it will be given to you. When we give to others, we live the fruit of the Spirit—charity (love).

Bitterness and Entitlement

One dreaded night, Jesus was on trial to be condemned to the cross. Peter found his way into the courtyard near where Jesus was

---

[6]*Wikipedia*, s.v. "Duty of Loyalty," http://1ref.us/kh (accessed August 3, 2017).

being interrogated. When Peter was recognized as a follower of Jesus, Peter denied it (or bore false witness). Jesus's response was sorrow. Peter recognized the goodness of God and turned from his false witness and with tears bore a true witness of the goodness of Jesus ... God (Matthew 26:69–75).

The ninth commandment says, "You shall not bear false witness against your neighbor" (Exod. 20:16). This is the law of the spoken word: How often, when we are bitter, do we express it in words? But the Bible says we are to speak to unify and strengthen. This law is also found in Ephesians 4:15, 25–32: "But speaking the truth in love ... laying aside falsehood, speak truth each one of you with his neighbor, for we are members of one another" (NASB). Let's consider our words, so we can receive the fruit of the Spirit—goodness.

Envy

James and John were brothers. One day, they had the idea that it would be good to continue to serve as brothers in eternity. So they asked Jesus if they could each sit beside Him on His throne. Jesus understood right away that this was not a selfish request. But the other ten disciples immediately became envious. Jesus responded that it was acts of service they should seek and not what belongs to another (Mark 10:35–45).

The tenth commandment says, "You shall not covet" (Exod. 20:17, NASB). This is the law of seeking: We need to seek for the pearl of great price and not seek what others have. This law is also found in the book of Matthew: "But seek first His kingdom and His righteousness, and all these things will be added to you" (Matt. 6:33, NASB). In order to keep this commandment, we must have the fruit of the Spirit—meekness.

These are the ten blessings—benefits—pronounced by God for those who choose Him to be their God. He longs for us to possess these blessings. God said that this is what we will be like if we have given ourselves to Him completely—these are the laws that will be written on our hearts and govern our lives. What is the best makeover ever? The one that God offers. The makeover of the heart is the cure for our wounds, and the surrender of the will to the Father is the prevention of sin. Christ's righteousness is the fruit of the Spirit returned to us. The will of the Father frees us from the cycle of hurting and being hurt.

The first part of healing the wilderness of the heart is doing a survey of the broken feelings that we experience. Are these hurts tied to a broken law of God? Can this insight help us find the way to follow Jesus? Eventually, we discover that the peace and joy and love and power that Jesus promised to give was there all along, sustaining us between broken moments.

Where do we stand? When we compare the secular with the sacred, it makes more sense to follow Jesus than to doubt. Even though humans have cast Him from the intimacy of their hearts, this same Yahshua Jesus remains nearby to guide and heal us of our sins and to show us how to remain free. His intent becomes even clearer when we see that the King of right remained true to us, even to the encounter with the cross. Jesus was willing to live everyday life. He was also willing to meet the cross and heal every kind of pain in our lives. This is Jesus's mission. Will we follow Him?

The Bible is a book of relationships with others and with God. So, we need to look at ourselves and how we relate to each other and the Almighty. We know more about putting things between us and our Father in heaven than we do about being comfortable around this great caregiver. Experiencing His power is more about removing things and ideas than it is about getting Him to do what we want. The Bible reveals the sin-induced pain in our lives in order that the sin may be removed by God, with our cooperation.

Emotional pain is a sign that there is sin nearby, because God gives only peace. The Word of God reveals to us that sin holds our lives captive. The longer you allow the root of bitterness to grow in the soil of your heart, the more love it will devour. The process may be painful and embarrassing, but trust in God and love for Jesus gives us the faith to hold still and be washed.

Check the emotions of brokenness that you want to delete from your response menu. These are the giants that need to be defeated by applying Jesus's blood of forgiveness and the fruit of the Spirit to yourself. Then you will receive the peace and authority that you may share with others. This is certainly not a conclusive study of how Jesus responded to our brokenness. But I hope it will encourage you to begin or continue the process of examining the thoughts and feelings that come out of your heart.

The Altar of Incense

Does having faith mean we don't need prayer? Are we asking, "Why do we need prayer when we have faith?" The Altar of Incense in the Holy Place represents our prayers.

I would like to suggest that without prayer, there is no faith. Forgiveness, praise, and thanksgiving: all these are elements of experience. But it is in relating to the Father by revealing our condition to Him as we see it that completes the process of faith. We may then accept and receive the application of His promises to this condition for ourselves or others.

Prayer is a safe place where we may be opened up to see what is really going on with us. When we speak to the Father of our condition, He *will* answer. This will include Him telling us what obstacles need to be removed and what needs to be added for our growth and character establishment. The best thing we can do for others is to pray about ourselves!

Where do we go in prayer? To the Father's throne. It is in the temple in heaven. It is where Jesus is ministering to heal our sin-ridden lives. Prayer opens the heart to God. We need not be embarrassed to let the Father know what we wish we could erase forever. He already knows. He is waiting to erase it, to throw it into the bottom of the sea (Micah 7:19).

> *The best thing we can do for others is to pray about ourselves!*

The anguish of our hearts receives a perfect response in the sanctuary of prayer. The foundation for our health is this acceptance from God. With every ounce of our being, we may speak to our Friend, the Father. There is nothing more purging than that. Jesus sweat great drops in earnest prayer to our Father. His Father is our Father and He is concerned with everything about us and still works tirelessly to save us.

A rose by any other name would smell as sweet. Prayer ascends with the intense saturation of the richest and best-blended incense to the throne of God. Is prayer to us like rich incense imbuing our being with the Word and a knowledge of the goodness of God? Do we have a yearning to make requests of faith, to know God's will that wounded souls may be healed? For this, we need to ask for the Spirit of grace and supplication, or we are resisting and quenching the will of God. If we don't ask, God must withhold His Spirit while He waits.

Within the pages of the Bible we will find the words to give us the yearning we desire:

> Our Father which art in heaven, Hallowed be Thy name.
> I shall not want when You
> Pour out on me the Spirit of grace and supplication.

Thy kingdom come, Thy will be done in earth, as
it is in heaven.
He makes me to lie down in green pastures:
He leads me beside the still waters. He restores my soul:
He leads me in the paths of righteousness for His name's sake.
Give us this day our daily bread.
Yea, though I walk through the valley of the shadow of death,
I will fear no evil: for Thou art with me; Thy rod and Thy staff,
they comfort me.
And forgive us our debts, as we forgive our debtors.
You prepare a table before me in the presence of mine enemies:
You anoint my head with oil;
my cup runs over.
I know that You do not lead us into temptation, but deliver us
from evil:
Yours is the kingdom, and the power, and the glory, forever.
Surely goodness and mercy shall follow me all the days of my life:
and I will dwell in the house of the Lord forever. Amen. Selah.

Praying in the morning is like setting the table for the day and warming up a thought pattern. It sets the agenda for the day. When you first begin to pray, open the Psalms to use as inspiration for your prayers. Your words may be short sentences. Don't get frustrated because you are not emotional enough. It is not a waste of time to be peaceful in prayer. In fact, let the Holy Spirit serve you the ideas. Allow yourself to be slowed down in processing information, so that you may be impressed by God. He does not poke us to get our attention. He rests His hand on us and gently moves us according to how pliable we become. It is in this way that we will yearn for the next appointment with our Friend. When you get up in the morning, you will be waiting on the next word from the Holy Spirit. As you receive your first assignment for the day, you will be charged with the goodness and life of the will of God.

In the evening and first thing in the morning, pray to do things God's way. Ask for wisdom. Revisit each problem in prayer with matching Bible verses. Saying the Word in prayer is salve for the heart. We must recognize the fruits of brokenness and apply the Word. Thus, we will reveal the fruits of the Spirit. When our hearts are healing, we are prepared to surrender the will to the Father to heal others.

Prayer can do anything God can do.[7] If we would do much for God, we must ask much of God. So, keep a prayer journal. It helps to see God's will at work, to recognize where you are needed, and to remember what you hope for!

In our interaction with others, we do anything to prevent our hearts or theirs from breaking. Would this be the will of the Father? By allowing self to be crucified and our hearts to break, we may be preserved from harmful indulgences, such as overeating or overspending. Praying burns away the dross of worldly thoughts and softens our hearts as we are reminded of the sweetness of the peace of God at the altar of incense.

How serious do we need to be when we pray? Let's look at Abraham's prayer for Lot (Gen. 18:16–33). He needed to pray for more than bodily deliverance. Abraham could have also prayed for Lot's and his family's hearts and wills. How often we neglect the weightier matters in prayer. Ask, "Is this a cry of the heart or an intellectual construction barricading the heart?"

It has been said you can't trust your emotions to act on them. Yes, we need to act on principle. Then deep and satisfying feelings or attitudes will follow. This applies to solving problems as well as

---

[7]R. A. Torrey, *The Power of Prayer and the Prayer of Power* (Mansfield Centre, CT: Martino Publishing, 2014).

preventing them. Then we may be healed by removing stumbling blocks, that our lives may grow in a new direction—toward God. All these are subjects for prayer.

Prayer with the Word is opening the heart to God and waiting for His will to be whispered in your ear. He reveals His will so we may know what to ask for. Prayer also gives us a time to concentrate on thanking God. This is our part of the covenant. Gratitude promotes Him to ourselves and those listening.

Chapter 3
The Way to Live

"I will rejoice greatly in the Lord, my soul will
exult in my God; for He has clothed me with
garments of salvation, He has wrapped me
with a robe of righteousness."
Isaiah 61:10 NASB

When we are patient in weakness, we may learn the will of the Father. Standing at the altar of incense, breathing in the thick fragrance of the oils of myrrh, frankincense, cinnamon, and calamus, and with the close encouragement of the Holy Spirit wafting through us, we utter the desire to be brought into the heightened security of the Most Holy Place. What is in the Most Holy Place that makes it special? What is it that provides and shows us about wellness?

It is the place we learn of the surrender of the will to Yahweh's authority as displayed at the cross. We learn even in subjection to evil that the Father may be trusted to save us: as He did His Son. He has the authority to care for us as represented by the budded branch, the manna, and the tables of stone written with the finger of God.

The works of our Messiah break our hearts. As our hearts of stone are broken at the sight of the service of His broken heart, our hearts are healed with His heart, we desire the will of the Father.

In the Most Holy Place, we find the angels with the glory over the ark with the mercy seat. Inside the ark, we discover the budded rod, the pot of manna, and the tablets of blessings written in stone.

The ark is the hope chest for the covenant between us and God: the almond branch, the manna, and the foundation written in stone. God is saying, "Let's try this again. Come out of the world of confusion. Please do what I tell you. I will give you the fruit of the tree of life, bread to eat and heavenly water from the river of life flowing from the throne!" How dear He is!

As we compare ourselves with the glory God intended for us, we identify conflicts of the will. We tend to suppress a sense of shame at our loss from doing things our way, instead of asking God to show us His will. Yet this creates stress. Pride and fear are the ways we exercise our will and deceive ourselves that we are in control; pride and fear create barriers between us and God (as well as us and other people). But our prayer needs to be, "Not my will but Yours, my Yahweh." It is God's will to give us authority, supply our daily needs, and bless us with closeness to Him and each other. Jesus is now in the Most Holy Place in heaven, working with us to do the Father's will. When all who will have joined together to do this, all heaven will break loose to come and get us, led by our divine Brother Himself!

As the heart is made up of thoughtful feelings and beliefs for relating, the will is made up of the desires and the conscience to protect us. It is with a clear conscience and holy desires that we are able to choose between right and wrong. It is time to live by the Father's will, not on our own.

The Hebrew Bible is a book of prophecies and promises about Jesus and could be referred to as a foundation. The Gospels and epistles are a revelation of the fulfillment of prophecy and the final call to a fallen world. The only thing that needs to be removed is the page separating the promise from the deliverance. The Bible is a book about God's will and whether we can trust it. It is to encourage us to make a covenant with Yahweh.

> *The Bible is a book about God's will and whether we can trust it.*

What is the covenant for? It is for us to be His people and for Him to be our God.

For this, we need the fruit of the Spirit and the application of His will to our experience. In this condition, we don't have as much damage control because we are living by understanding instead of with defensive maneuvers.

What is necessary for victory? Ask yourself this question: "As a believer, do I really need to defend myself, be deceived by traditions, or be divided from the peace of God?" As you proceed to surrender as an apprentice of the will of Yahweh, you will appreciate the Word and its ability to prepare the will. All learning doesn't have to be by trial and error. We may learn from other people's mistakes and Another's rightness.

The Ark of the Covenant

The contents of the Ark of the Covenant speak to the provision God has given for us to make it in this world.

The Pot of Manna

God's will is to provide our daily bread to take care of us physically. The Bible truly reveals that we may seek first the kingdom of God and all else will be added to us (Matt. 6:33). Our doubt began in the Garden of Eden when a meal was preferred over intimacy with God. Today, we may end the doubt and trust God even as we are spent to serve.

The Budded Almond Rod

God's will is that we have authority over spiritual things by the grace of His Holy Spirit. We learn about the authority and power of God by observing creation. The power of God is the power of life: to change the lifeless into the fruitful. "Not by might, nor by power, but by my spirit," says Yahweh (Zech. 4:6, KJV).

In chapters 38–40 of Job, God takes Job on a tour of nature and asks him questions about Job's ability to deal with the deep requirements of nature and humankind. Gradually, these chapters draw the picture of a vastly complicated, intricately intertwined universe for which is required a heart of gold and a will for justice to direct all the activities needed to resolve the questions on which eternity hangs.[8]

---

[8]Stedman, Ray. "Job: The Hardest Lesson." June 13, 1965. Ray Stedman.org: Authentic Christianity. http://1ref.us/m5 (accessed September 19, 2017).

Creation speaks to us of the Maker as a trustworthy director and guide as well as the Source of life. We need to draw from this Source today more than ever. Is it suppression or growth that we want? I mean real growth that includes healthy emotions and doesn't just attempt to deny, empty, or entertain our broken emotions. Remember, if we are a friend of the world, we are an enemy of God (James 4:4). Our God-given emotions of the fruit of the Spirit (love, joy, peace, patience, kindness, goodness, faithfulness, gentleness, self-control) are the original sin-free emotions we were meant to have and enjoy. It is only from God that we may draw life by partaking of the fruit of the Spirit. This fruit possesses the fingerprints of God, the golden ratio, the look of love bound by law. This is what we ultimately need to be predictably safe. Works without the will of God are destructive.

God is the Ruler of the vast universe, yet we find in His heart tender love that cares for His wayward children patiently and gently on this tiny speck of a world. He meant for us not to experience brokenness and pain but to partake only of the fruit of His Spirit. This is to where all history points. Jesus calls us to be single-minded, not double-minded by doubt. Yes, this is overwhelming to think about. But we find help in the study of the book called the Bible.

God is calling us to be like Him. Do we hear the sound of Him in the Garden of Eden, saying, "Where are you?" (Gen. 3:9, NASB). Where are we? Do you know where you are? God needed to call for Adam and Eve because they had left Him by partaking of the tree of the knowledge of good and evil. The fruit was good for food, but the serpent was evil and took captive Adam's and Eve's wills.

How can we be free from the fruits of brokenness and confusion? The answer is to be found by living the will of God, not by human nature. This is what will shake the Earth to its core to separate the wheat from the tares for the great harvest. Remember, don't be surprised when the last are first and the first are last—this is the way of love.

Two groups of humanity were first demonstrated in the lives of Cain and Abel. Cain demonstrated the result of continuing to follow the serpent and distrust God's directions. Abel accepted that he was a servant of sacrifice gladly as it was the way to be free from the curses of sin. In these two groups, we see the prosecution and the defense of God on trial. Do we want an escape from God, or do we want a bridge to cover the gap between us and the Almighty? The Bible presents the case for the goodness of God and shows us the way to own His fruitful authority.

The Stone Tablets

The Father's will is to bless us with happiness. We read that we should seek first the things of heaven and all else will be added to us (Matt. 6:33). God also wants to protect us from shame, anger, and loneliness. How do we give permission to these feelings? We do this by breaking laws that the Father established to connect us with Him. When we ask God to set these boundaries around us, it prevents pain.

As a parent has authority over a child, so the Father has authority over us. He is responsible for bringing us into existence, and He sustains our life moment by moment. When we understand His laws, we will begin to know God. The expression of His very nature—His thoughts, feelings, and desires—is found in His laws. When we defy these laws, we defy love. The following is a scripture poem that reveals the tender nature of the God of the Ten Commandments. This beautiful character is the very thing He wants to share with us.

"I am the Alpha and the Omega," says the Lord God, "who is, and who was, and who is to come, the Almighty." (Rev. 1:8, NIV)

Is there any God besides Me, or, is there any other Rock? I know of none. (Isaiah 44:8, NASB)

Come unto me, all ye that labour and are heavy laden, and I will give you rest. Take my yoke upon you, and learn of me; for I am meek and lowly in heart: and ye shall find rest unto your souls. For my yoke is easy, and my burden is light. (Matt. 11:28–30, KJV)

Let the one who is thirsty come; let the one who wishes take the water of life without cost. (Rev. 22:17, NASB)

"Let him come to Me and drink." (John 7:37, NASB)

Blessed are they which do hunger and thirst after righteousness: for they shall be filled. (Matt. 5:6, KJV)

Keeping the Ten Commandments in our hearts will fill us with such goodness that all our needs and desires will always be met because we trust in the Author of these laws. Each of the Ten Commandments speaks simply and clearly. Sinful, finite humans can easily understand God's laws. Yet, there is a foundational law that applies to the vast workings of a sinless universe at the root of each commandment. If you are looking for joy, behold God; if you are looking for peace, keep the Sabbath.

The Ten Commandments start with the four laws of worship and finish with the six laws of behavior. We certainly need laws to govern our worship, especially as we near the end of time. In our "anything goes" society, it is easy to confuse self-worship with the real worship of God. We were perfectly designed by God, but when sin came into the world, it damaged God's handiwork. Without His guidance, we are easily led into false worship.

In reading the commandments, I realize that a specific fruit of the Spirit was the result of keeping each one. It is not from *our* keeping the law, because that is impossible now. Christ is the one who lived the spirit of the law in all its subtleties.

Chapter 4
In His Image

"We have seen today that God speaks with man,
yet he lives."
Deuteronomy 5:24 NASB

There remains one more question for the apprentice. It is a question of identity. Since this is a book about receiving the image of God, we must look at this subject. Let us now dust off the antique concept of male and female. We are made male and female in the image of God. No matter what else we do, we have a fundamental role that is a part of our walk in life.

God's people in the Old Testament were also called a "kingdom of priests" (Exod. 19:6, KJV). Even so, they had a tribe of priests set aside for functions that only the priests could perform. We all have access to the spiritual gifts and fruit. Yet there are "differences of administrations" and "diversities of operations" (1 Cor. 12:4–7, KJV).

We all receive honor or shame apart from our gifts. This is based on character, not gifts.

We all have the joy of giving others a tour of this glorious plan of restoring our personal temples to the presence of God. Yet, even as Moses led the great assembly in the wilderness, the congregations of today are to be led and protected by the image of God as represented by the men: elders and deacons. The system of patriarchal authority as found in the Bible is not to be feared but to be enjoyed. It is a shelter, a guidepost, and a pattern for the home.

Jesus came to reveal the Father. This is our ministry also. There is a cry for the Word, a cry for the Spirit. The final cry will be for the Father, Abba. How much more important for the Eves of the world to cry, "Abba, Father." This is where His tie with humanity was broken. Women, we have a special place in the heart of the Father that only we can fill.

> *Jesus came to reveal the Father. This is our ministry also.*

As Peter describes in his first letter, we are to be "a chosen people, a royal priesthood, a holy nation" (1 Peter 2:9, NIV).

A priesthood of believers is not now a free-for-all. It is a nation, an organized, orderly people. A holy nation means with the model of authority ordained by Yahweh. This model is the patriarchal system used in the Bible.

As men are to return to the Shepherd and Overseer of their beings, Paul goes on to say, "Wives, submit yourselves to your own husbands as you do to the Lord" (Eph. 5:22, NIV). This is the essence of what identifies the holy kingdom: the subjection to authority, the holy hierarchy. As there are principalities and powers in the realm of darkness seeking control, let it be seen what principles the true kingdom is run by and what fuels the power of holiness. It is the very patriarchal system of authority, surrendering control, that distinguishes us from the world around us. Without that, we become Babylon.

Do you hear the call to come out of Babylon? Babylon is confusion. Confusion has no order. Order needs a hierarchy of authority. God's kingdom is not made up of the will of the majority. It is constructed by the will of the Father: the order of the home; the true Shepherd, father, mother, child.

The authority of God is based on submission rather than control. Whether or not we are a father or mother, we are a child or a neighbor and the kingdom of heaven may reach others through us—through our submission to others and our precious God. The Holy Spirit writes on our hearts the works of Christ that we may do the will of the Father. Through submission, we experience the atonement supplied by our covenant with Yahweh God.

> *The authority of God is based on submission rather than control.*

This is the shaking that will shake us to the core. Who will stand for the image of God or His instructions? The time has come to witness for the sacrifice of Christ, for the work of His hands: man and woman. We can do this by faith.

We all receive the fruit of the Spirit equally. This may be used as the Spirit leads. This is the high calling. In order for the covenant to be completed, the image of God needs to have a witness—not only the fruit of the Spirit but the submissive male and female. This is where the sin problem started and this is where it will end.

Men won't value women because they don't act like men. Women expect men to treat them the way women treat men, and nobody does their job. Adam and Eve both broke from their unique identities and authorities—from freedom—to a common authority of enslavement: Satan. There is no uniqueness under Satan's rule, only a dreadful commonality of separation from God and each other. This ends in disruption of all life's laws and processes to return into the dust of the earth.

We need to submit to God and each other as Christ submitted to the needs of the church and the will of the Father. Marriage reflects this image of God. It is the institution that Yahweh has assigned to represent the orderly, blessed interaction of male and female.

You cannot have submission without authority and vice versa. This is the very core of the definition of male and female. Without it, you don't have the image of God. Although women submit to men's leadership as such, they are every bit reflecting the image and glory of God, even as the man is submitting to Jesus. If all of us want to speak with the authority of the King of kings, we must accept His organization or government. The everlasting kingdom runs on respect and nurturing. Without those, we are like the thief trying to get in another way who will be cast out.

It must be shown that humanity can reflect the image of God in male and female: that Eve accepts the headship of a Christ-like man and the role of humility. Christ humbled Himself by death on a cross. The Father is humbled by giving all to the Son. The Holy Spirit is humble and does the will of the Father and glorifies the Son. The man is humbled under Christ. Why should woman be the only one that is not humbled? Women's leadership sustains the lot of fallen woman. Eve was made to be a help to Adam. If she had stayed within her role, she would never have talked to the serpent. So it is today. Modern Eves only continue to strengthen the ways of the enemy by refusing to listen to a Higher Authority and doing as they think best. Women should not be pastors, because it does not follow the divine plan of line of authority. There is a good reason for this line of authority: it is a protection for the man and the woman—to keep them both humble. As a pastor, woman loses the authority of love, the authority of submission as found in God's Word. We need more watchmen sounding the trumpets of judgment and women witnessing to the authority of submission. This is where the case rests.

Chapter 5
The Father's Will

"Blessed are they who do hunger and thirst after righteousness for they shall be filled."
Matthew 5:6

The Father is the origin of all authority, judgment, and direction: the Ruler that gives us rest. When we let Him rule in our lives, we have rest from our own ideas and efforts and trust in His already established authority. This is true peace.

First and foremost, we need His authority to help us in relationships. Do you find it difficult to grow in character, to become close to God and others? Discard the evidence of any other spiritual authority.

God was the father of Isaac, who was in turn the father of Jacob, and so on. You can follow this line from Jesse to David and to our Jesus. God's answer to our confusion and loss of sense of direction is the same that it was nearly four thousand years ago—fathers! What is needed are men who will teach and rule the truth so we may learn how to live by honor instead of the default—shame.

To rule means to guard, protect, and direct. If you are under the authority of a man who has refused this honor and chosen shame, you may still seek the place where this spiritual covering may be found—the assembly or church with a pastor and elders. Don't be like me, hanging around in an abusive marriage because you think it is the Christian thing to do. For your sake and your children's sake, *leave*! No matter how bleak it seems, God will start pouring blessings out as soon as you are gone from the abuser. (There is a lot more to be said about this. But it will have to wait till the next book.) Women are not the only ones who need the covering of patriarchal authority—men and children need it as well.

Patriarchal authority is founded on the goodness of the Father in heaven. It is He who orders all Creation. Surely, He knows best. We may have the same order in our lives. For this, we need deliverance from that which creates confusion. We receive guidance, which delivers us by encouraging us to seek the Father's will in every aspect of our lives. This is the answer to relentless pride, relentless shame, or relentless rejection. God's will is not a lofty, obscure path to some form of oblivion. It is focused on us: loving us out from behind our walls of bondage. Yes, the Father's will accomplishes many purposes. But all He asks of us is to believe He loves us. Believe enough to live the life of Yahshua Jesus.

There are ancient roots of our faith that are necessary for the deep experience we seek with the Father. Jesus understood these roots and they are also meant for us. In these last days, when our bodies are to be restored for holy use, there is an awakening on these subjects.

God's will is not a lofty, obscure path to some form of oblivion. It is focused on us: loving us out from behind our walls of bondage.

The study of the Bible must also be about digging out the ancient concepts that are the setting for understanding the significance of the promises of God. They are also critical for the authority of belief to resist wrong and to know the Father's will.

Ancient Roots of the Good News

The Bible declares the omnipotent, omnipresent, immutable, omniscient, eternal nature of God. This is the foundation for our beliefs. Accepting this is what prepares us for victory.

Honor and Shame

The concepts of honor and shame are important to understand. They are an integral part of temptation losing its power. Where do we get a sense of honor from? Is it from our past accomplishments in the life of sin? Or the present humility of entrusting our honor to the will of the Father? When we are in a tempting situation, do we recognize the presentation of honor or shame? Do we recognize this as a temptation? Do we accept the peace and humility of the Father as our badge of honor?[9]

The Royal Messenger

It is not just prophecy dates that identify the Son of God. It is the fulfillment of His roles, and for this, we must understand the ancient roots. The coming of the Son of God is the culmination of the history and deliverance spoken of in the Book of life.

The royal-messenger theme adds living color to our understanding of the rich tapestry of Jesus's life. Although the deceiver has counterfeited everything that is true, the empire of this world and the kingdom of God have nothing in common.[10]

Yahweh doesn't miss a chance to make an appointment with us. Every kind of time is draped with significance and remembrance that God knows how to care and has made provision for you. Meet with Him and be blessed by His presence. Remove the obstacles between you and Yahweh. These divine appointments are daily, weekly, monthly, and seasonal!

Limited Good versus Everlasting Blessing

The Father has the authority to bless forever and without limit.[11] There is no limit to His goodness. Replay the places of pain in your life with your earthly father with how it should have been done by the goodness of the heavenly Father. This will heal the

---

[9]Daniel McGirr, "The Kingdom Concept of Honor and Shame," Ancient Covenant Ministries, http://1ref.us/k8 (accessed August 3, 2017).
[10]Daniel McGirr, "The Royal Messenger," Ancient Covenant Ministries, http://1ref.us/k8 (accessed August 3, 2017).
[11]Daniel McGirr, "The Parable of the Talents and its Limited Good Context," Ancient Covenant Ministries, http://1ref.us/k8 (accessed August 3, 2017).

wound of betrayal. The experience will help you look at the Father for who He really is.

God is the author of direction, the authority for blessing. A pagan is someone who tries to fix things on their own, without God's will. Instead, let an understanding of the ancient roots reveal the Father's will. Break the chains that you may begin to experience true free will—the will of the Father, the will to live your destiny.

Chapter 6
The Heart Made Flesh

*"The Lord's lovingkindnesses indeed never cease,
for His compassions never fail. They are new
every morning; Great is your faithfulness."
Lamentations 3:22,23 NASB*

To take our hearts from withered to alive, the heart of God was made flesh. When God asks for our worship, it is not asking very much. It is only an agreement that He is worth something. We may connect with God by acknowledging His worth. This is true worship. It sounds easy because it is!

It is Jesus that makes this worship possible. Think for a minute. Where would we be if Jesus had not come down to Earth? We would never have heard the Golden Rule (Luke 6:31). We would not be able to experience love, joy, peace, gentleness, or self-control. Yes, God is good.

In the temple, we discover that the only way to come to the Father is by the Son. We learn of the baptisms of water and fire in the outer court. In the Holy Place, we see the blood sprinkled on the inner veil. This reminds us that the only way to the Father's blessings is through the price that Christ paid with His baptism of blood. Why do we want to get to the Father? Because His will is the essence of love. It is from Him that the streams of living love flow.

It was not only access to the throne of God but access to the heart of man that Jesus's broken flesh accomplishes. His blood cleanses us from the inside that we may receive the Holy Spirit and the fruit of the Spirit. Christ's works made it possible for us to change our minds from sin to holy while still in the context of free will. The example of Christ was the only thing that would change our minds within the boundaries of free will. It is free will that must prevail, not seduction and deceit. Christ supplies the way. The disciples are to receive the great fruit of the Holy Spirit and implement the will of the Father.

The high priest had the names of the tribes, both on his shoulders and on his breast, which reminds us of the authority of love with which our Jesus pleads for those that are His. This hope sustains the heart. Our Messiah Jesus is the author and finisher of our faith in the Father and of our acceptance with the Father. For this, it was necessary that He be made flesh.

Because God was made flesh, we have the same choice Adam and Eve had: to be tenderhearted with loving God and our neighbors or to be focused on ourselves. We are born with a heart of stone; but because of Jesus, we may receive a heart of life. Our freedom does not end with the new heart. The choice and the freedom remain as we, with our new heart, willingly cut off the sins that have made us who we are. It is not the plan for us, with our new heart, to suffocate the heart with bad lungs or choke out the life with damaged digestion. Jesus sacrificed His body with a broken heart, broken by doing the will of the Father. Are we obeying God's will for sacrifice? He brought heaven to Earth. He was the link that allowed the Holy Spirit to associate with us. He brought the Holy Spirit with Him into the realm of sinful humanity.

Jesus's life showed us that our sinful flesh must be surrendered, moved by the will of the Father, and consumed by the fiery Spirit, that we may bear the heart of God. We must learn to surrender the body to service when we are weak: doing His will is the only thing that gives us the strength to go forward. Wait for His strength, then you will know His will.

> *We are born with a heart of stone; but because of Jesus, we may receive a heart of life.*

Chapter 7
Walk With the Spirit

"Restore to me the joy of Your salvation and sustain me with a willing spirit."
Psalm 51:12 NASB

The effect of the Holy Spirit is not political power or the power of the state to control. This Spirit is blessedness that molds us by eroding the clots of pain in our lives. Let us allow ourselves to be impressed with holy things, not with unclean things. The unholy are not really spiritual because these things take away our breath and promote loss, not life.

The Spirit's fruit fills the gaping voids in our lives. Walk with the Spirit, not with the world. Who is the Holy Spirit? A breeze? Just like water is structured, there is structure to the Holy Spirit: a structure founded on the Ten Commandments. This is a Person of infinite beauty who draws us to the essential Word. If we are not drawn to the Word, is it because we are being influenced by the delusions of the world?

Study the Bible, ask questions. The Holy Spirit interacts with us to find the answer. The Holy Spirit is our source of communication, peace, and comfort. The fiery, living fruit of the Spirit is delivered to the cleansed ground of our repentant hearts. With the fruit of the Spirit, we have hope. Enough hope to begin to care.

We need the Holy Spirit to turn our lives upside down and inside out. Otherwise, we continue to stumble, lonely, from one destination of our own devising to another. "Beloved, think it not strange concerning the fiery trial which is to try you" (1 Peter 4:12, KJV). Patiently wait on Him. Rest in His promises. Become strong, that you may discover God's purposes: your destiny.

> *We need the Holy Spirit to turn our lives upside down and inside out.*

Conclusion

Will today bring works of knowledge or the fruit of life from the Spirit? The purpose of Bible study and prayer is to experience worship. This is the presence of God: God with us. This is where the flow of living water begins. Without it, all we have is works and no fruit.

We reject the Messiah because we think He came to rule our wills. He came to win our hearts. When we are born again, what is it that we are born into? A kingdom. A kingdom has a king. We are born into a kingdom with Yahshua Jesus as King. The kingdom also includes the involvement of the Father and the Spirit: the will of the Father and the support of the Spirit. This is the way of life that results in everlastingness. This pattern gives us a fundamental understanding of our mighty Godhead and the kind of give and take They have. This draws us from the comatose to the conscious—it helps us to wake up and see that God is worthy of worship. He is easier to understand than we thought.

> *We reject the Messiah because we think He came to rule our wills. He came to win our hearts.*

Every king has a seal. Of course, the King of kings has a seal. A seal consists of three components: the name, the authority or mode of power, and the territory. The born-again experience has these three components: the name or identity of Yahshua Jesus in our hearts, the authority of the sacrifice, and the territory—us. Each room of the temple applies this seal deeper into our being, until we are surrendered to His presence and ignited with God's love.

The plan of salvation or covenant is to be born of the Spirit, healed in the heart by Yahshua so that we may surrender the will to the Father. This is displayed in the outer court, the Holy Place, and the Most Holy Place of the temple.

By confession (i.e., the name), forgiveness (i.e., the authority), and presence (i.e., the territory), we are sealed as citizens of the kingdom of heaven. It is this pattern that is the foundation, the blueprint for the covenant with God.

> The Spirit and the bride say, Come.
> (Rev. 22:17, KJV)

> This is my covenant with them, when I take away their sins.
> (Rom. 11:27, NASB)

> A new covenant, not of the letter but of the Spirit; for the letter kills but the Spirit gives life.
> (2 Cor. 3:6, NASB)

> Many will be purged, purified and refined, but the wicked will act wickedly; and none of the wicked will understand, but those who have insight will understand.
> (Dan. 12:10, NASB)

It is my prayer that this book will help to usher in the soon-coming kingdom of everlasting goodness, where we will never exhaust the studies begun under the limits of time. Today is the day to get ready and enlist as an apprentice of the Almighty.

We all like to have something new. It is clean and refreshing and puts us in a good mood. It is not just things that can be new, but also thoughts, feelings, and desires! I want to share this poem with you.

Smile

Like a bread without the spreadin',
Like a puddin' without sauce,
Like a mattress without beddin',
Like a cart without a hoss,
Like a door without a latchstring,
Like a fence without a stile,
Like a dry an' barren creek bed—
Is the face without a smile.
Like a house without a dooryard,
Like a yard without a flower,
Like a clock without a mainspring
That will never tell the hour,
A thing that sort o' makes yo' feel
A hunger all the while—
Oh, the saddest sight that ever was
Is a face without a smile.
The face of man was built for smiles,
An' thereby he is blest
Above the critters of the field,
The birds an' all the rest;
He's just a little lower
Than the angels in the skies,
An' the reason is that he can smile;
Therein his glory lies!
So smile an' don't forget to smile,
An' smile, an' smile agin;

'Twill help you all along the way, an' cheer you mile by mile:
An' so, whatever is your lot,
Jes' smile, an' smile, an' smile.
(Author Unknown)

Bibliography

Costella, Dennis. "The Fiery Trial." *Foundation Magazine*. May–June 1996.

DeYoung, Kevin. "Who Can Baptize?" The Gospel Coalition. http://1ref.us/k7 (accessed August 3, 2017).

McGirr, Daniel. Ancient Covenant Ministries. http://1ref.us/k8 (accessed August 3, 2017).

Northrop, Chuck. "Fruit of the Spirit Articles by Chuck Northrop." Lee & Walnut Church of Christ. http://1ref.us/k9 (accessed August 3, 2017).

Stedman, Ray. "Job: The Hardest Lesson." June 13, 1965. Ray Stedman.org: Authentic Christianity. http://1ref.us/m5 (accessed September 19, 2017).

"The Almond Rod: Redemption of Humanity." Straight Talk About God. http://1ref.us/ka (accessed August 3, 2017).

Torrey, R. A. *The Power of Prayer and the Prayer of Power*. Mansfield Centre, CT: Martino Publishing, 2014.

We invite you to view the complete
selection of titles we publish at:

www.TEACHServices.com

Scan with your mobile
device to go directly
to our website.

Please write or e-mail us your praises, reactions, or
thoughts about this or any other book we publish at:

TEACH Services, Inc.
P U B L I S H I N G
www.TEACHServices.com • (800) 367-1844

11 Quartermaster Circle
Fort Oglethorpe, GA 30742

info@TEACHServices.com

TEACH Services, Inc., titles may be purchased in bulk for
educational, business, fund-raising, or sales promotional use.
For information, please e-mail:

BulkSales@TEACHServices.com

Finally, if you are interested in seeing
your own book in print, please contact us at

publishing@TEACHServices.com

We would be happy to review your manuscript for free.

www.ingramcontent.com/pod-product-compliance
Lightning Source LLC
Chambersburg PA
CBHW040227180426
43200CB00026BA/2954